VOYAGE, WAR, EXILE

ETEL ADNAN

VOYAGE, WAR, EXILE

THREE ESSAYS

WITH DRAWINGS
BY SIMONE FATTAL

LITMUS PRESS
NEW YORK

Cover image and interior drawings by Simone Fattal
Design and typesetting by Kit Schluter

Litmus Press is a program of Ether Sea Projects, Inc., a 501(c)(3) non-profit literature and arts organization.

Litmus Press publications are made possible by the New York State Council on the Arts with support from Governor Kathy Hochul and the New York State Legislature. Additional support for Litmus Press comes from the Leslie Scalapino–O Books Fund, The Post-Apollo Press, individual members and donors. All contributions are fully tax-deductible.

ISBN: 978-1-933959-77-1

LCCN: 2024007861

Cataloging-in-Publication data is available from the Library of Congress.

LITMUS PRESS
925 Bergen Street #405
Brooklyn, New York 11238
litmuspress.org

All Litmus Press titles are distributed by ASTERISM BOOKS
asterismbooks.com

CONTENTS

TO WRITE IN A FOREIGN LANGUAGE (1984)

LANGUAGES START AT HOME; SO I WILL START with the history of my involvement with many languages and with the way the use of languages which were not the ones I should have normally spoken or used in writing poetry and prose, affected me. I will start with some information about my own family's background, and its own struggles on the same theme.

My mother was a Greek from Smyrna, when Smyrna, before World War I, was a predominantly Greek city, a Greek speaking community within the Ottoman Empire. My father was an Arab. He was born in Damascus, Syria. At the age of twelve he joined the Military Academy in Istanbul, called the War College. That was close to the end of the nineteenth century. Damascus was a part of the Ottoman Empire, and my father was an Ottoman officer. Turkey being then an ally of the Kaiser's Germany, my father got training in Turkish, German, and French, besides his earlier studies in Arabic. French was taught in the Ottoman Empire for general education, for the same reasons that it was also taught in Russia.

My father, who was a Moslem, married my mother who, much younger than him, also represented a different culture. This was at the beginning of World War I, somewhere around 1916. So I was told. They spoke Turkish together; the Greeks, living in Turkey, all knew some Turkish and spoke Greek only at home and in their schools. Their lives were very close to their church, and culture and religion were intertwined. There were extremely few marriages outside one's culture-group.

The Ottoman Empire was an "empire," which meant it was not a state with a unified group of people. It was an empire in which Turkish was not even the most spoken language. Turkish itself was a language full of Arabic words and expressions, because the Turks, being Moslems, learned the Koran in Arabic. There were also Armenians in the Empire who spoke Armenian, as well as Turkish. So almost everybody knew at least a bit of another language besides their own; but everyone was rooted in their community, language, and life.

So, as I said, my parents had Turkish as a common language. My mother had gone to a convent school until she was twelve; the French had convents in all the major cities, and the "educated" people learned French. Some French, at least. So my parents understood French, knew how to read and write it. My mother spoke, but did not study, Turkish. So when my father was on the

Dardanelles front, close to Istanbul, for quite a while and through a major battle, he wrote letters to her in French. His language was romantic, in the tone of the German, Austrian, or Russian novels of the time. Many years later, because these letters were carefully kept and were my mother's pride and joy, I read them. They could have been written within a work like Tolstoy's *War and Peace*: they spoke of love, of war, of life and of death. They were written under the sound of the cannons, in black ink and a handwriting that drew the letters of the alphabet very clearly. They are lost today, because of the too many moves I made in my life, and the carelessness of my younger days.

I was born in Beirut, Lebanon, because at the end of World War I my parents left Turkey and came to settle in Beirut. Beirut was close to Damascus, my father's home. Many years later, I was born in a world totally different from the one my parents knew. The Allies had occupied the Arab East and had divided it; the French kept for themselves a region they sub-divided into Syria and Lebanon. They immediately started in Lebanon a network of French schools run by French priests, brothers, and nuns.

Thus, I went to a French convent school and was educated in French. The children of my generation saw a country ruled by French people who enjoyed for themselves, and their language and customs, the prestige always attributed to Power. We were taught the same books as the French kids in Europe, the capital of the world seemed to be Paris, and we learned the names of all kinds of things we never heard or saw: French rivers, French mountains, the history of blue-eyed people who had built an empire. The French nuns whose families had just suffered an invasion from the Kaiser's armies hated the Germans and passed on to us the hatred of German . . . and so on. Somehow we breathed an air where it seemed that being French was superior to anyone, and as we were obviously not French, the best thing was at least to speak French. Little by little, a whole generation of educated boys and girls felt superior to the poorer kids who did not go to school and spoke only Arabic. Arabic was equated with backwardness and shame. Years later I learned that the same thing was happening all over the French empire, in Morocco, Algeria, Tunisia, Black Africa and Indochina.

The method used to teach French to the children was in itself a kind of a psychological conditioning against which nobody objected, the people thinking that whatever nuns do is always good and for the best: so there was a system in all the French-run schools which charged a few selected students to "spy" on the others: anybody heard in class or in recreation speaking Arabic was punished and a little stone was immediately put into the pocket of that child; speaking Arabic was equated with the notion of sin. Most of the students spoke Arabic at home, but when they themselves became parents they started talking in either French or Arabic to their own children, or a mixture of the two languages.

Going back to my own childhood: as early as I can remember I spoke Greek and Turkish until I was about five years old, the time I went to school. The fact that at school I spoke French, and that there were French residents in the city—some of them neighbors with whom my mother used the French she herself had learned in Smyrna in her childhood—made us as a family use French at home more and more: my mother happily, my father reluctantly. And there were reasons for that: my father was an Arab in an Arab country and spoke Arabic in his dealings in town or with his friends. My mother, not knowing Arabic, identified somewhat with the French people, although she never thought that being a Greek made her similar to them. No, she only knew their language, imperfectly, and used it, and started to use it also with me, the only child of her marriage.

I remember my father, who was an old man for the child I was and looked rather like the grandparents of the other kids, once in a while, like somebody getting out of a dream, start suddenly to get worried and say to my mother things along these lines: "we are not in

France, and all this French speaking is not right. This child should learn Arabic." She would reply: "Why don't you teach her?" and he would keep silent, or say a few words in Arabic, words that seemed to be swallowed up by the whole house.

When I was six or seven I remember my father had a fountain pen which he liked particularly; once in a while he had to fill out administrative papers, and since Arabic was the official language, he wrote, in a regular and distinguished way, lines and lines in a language which was for me neither foreign nor familiar. He taught me the Arabic alphabet, and made me copy it maybe a hundred times. I used to draw the letters with application.

Then, for a short while, he used an old Arabic-Turkish grammar that had survived his own adventurous life. He was proud of telling me that it was the very Arabic-Turkish grammar he had used at the Military Academy as a cadet: the book was thick, narrow, with yellowish pages, and its cover much written over. I learned in it to decline verbs, and short sentences which explained the use of the verb forms. Sometimes I was bored, or distracted; he used to scold me gently, but he used to lose his own patience very quickly, and using my mother as a witness he would say: "it's hopeless, the schools should be doing that, and these nuns are propagandists. Everything is propaganda in this country!"

Tired of giving unscheduled lessons, and perhaps, and more seriously, because of being a man vanquished in the war, a witness to the end of an empire for which he fought, got wounded and decorated, this Ottoman officer was not a pedagogue: he told me one day to sit and copy the grammar book, page after page: "copy these lessons, he told me, and you will learn Arabic."

So I remember that once in a while (did it last one year, two years, a single season? I can't tell) I used to sit and copy—which means reproduce faithfully, words after words whose alphabet I understood, but seldom their meaning—never trying to understand what I was writing: I think that I loved the act of writing things I did not understand, and I pretended that I was learning a language without effort, just by writing it down. There must have been something hypnotizing about these exercises because much later, and for different reasons, I ended up doing practically the same thing. Of this I will speak later.

Copying a language I didn't know did not make me learn Arabic; and living in a school where Arabic was the forbidden thing made me feel very alone and want to give it up. My father inadvertently helped; he said one day, maybe out of nostalgia for his student days at the War College—I remember this very clearly, because by then I must have been about ten years old—he said that the future of the world was in the sciences and particularly chemistry, and that he would send me when I grew up to Germany to study and be a chemist. Was I happy to dream of such an extraordinary thing, or was it an ideal excuse not to study Arabic? All I know is that when, a few years later, under the pressure of the Government, the French schools started to teach a course in Arabic for two hours a week, I went up to the Mother Superior of the school and told her that as I was going to Germany some day to study I didn't need to take the course. She said that was all right, if that was what my parents thought. So I took Latin with the French born children and never went beyond the first chapters. Spring in Beirut made children troublesome and summer followed very quickly; extra studies like Latin, drawing, sewing, and botany never went very far with anybody. And as for adding Arabic! Arabic became a second class language within its own country.

When World War II erupted I was in secondary school. I saw the city of Beirut become an internationally important city. The French and British armies had headquarters in it, and the cosmopolitan character of the place glittered with a special romanticism for which movies had prepared us. To a population which included communities of Greeks, Italians, Kurds, and Armenians, besides the native population, were added troops of different nationalities making up the Allied armies: Australians, Canadians, New Zealanders, Black Africans, Free Poles.

Beirut became a microcosm, a little tornado of war and fun. It did not see real war, but the armies which were tearing the world apart.

For the little girl I was, that meant "new" faces, new "happenings," new languages. We became conscious of the "importance" of the English language, and some Lebanese families who were familiar with Alexandria and Cairo, who had lived there and had come back, brushed up the English they spoke just to be in the stream of History. The American University of Beirut, which had mainly foreign students, started increasing its Lebanese student body. The city which was bilingual was becoming trilingual. When, in fact, about ten years later the Palestinian refugees came to Lebanon, the most educated among them knew Arabic and English and a whole business section of the city, close to the American University, used English and not French as a commercial language.

Universities create cultural areas around them and Beirut revolved around three universities that represented three cultures, three ways of life, three intellectual options, I would say three destinies. And as expected, writers, literary magazines, even newspapers, followed the trend. It was of course a kind of wealth, an opening onto the world, a thrilling diversity. But it also created, in a country too small to easily absorb such a strong wind of change and cultural pulling apart, undercurrents of tensions that were to explode a generation later and practically destroy it.

Little by little, Lebanon developed an intense cultural life, but this was fragmented into linguistic groups: there were major poets (like Georges Schéhadé), writing in French; most were still writing in Arabic, and there were writers, poets and journalists writing in English. For a country of three million people such a phenomenon considerably reduced the audience for each group. It was a genuine problem. A poet or a writer never had the feeling that he or she was addressing himself or herself to the nation as a whole. I was writing in French. I started writing poetry at the age of twenty: it was a long poem that I called "Le Livre de la Mer," "The Book of the Sea," a poem which sees the interrelation between the sun and the sea as a kind of cosmic eroticism. But even here, later on, the fact that the poem was written in French presented me with a problem. My work in poetry is generally translated into Arabic and published in the two or three most important Arab literary magazines. "The Book of the Sea" is not yet translated for the very reason that the sea, as a noun, in French, is feminine, and the sun is a masculine word. In Arabic it is the contrary: the whole poem is developed along the metaphor of the sea being a woman and the sun a warrior, or a masculine principle. So the poem is not only not translatable, it is, in a genuine sense, unthinkable in Arabic.

In the early fifties I went to Paris to study philosophy at the Sorbonne and wrote some poetry. I met American students at the Cité Universitaire and after a short trip back to Beirut, I landed in New York in January 1955, and a few months later Berkeley, California. I did not realize that changing universities was not just continuing one's studies elsewhere. It was a total subversion of one's own thinking, a little earthquake in a student's life. Going from the Sorbonne to the University of California in Berkeley, in 1955, was like changing planets. Knowing four languages already, more or less efficiently, was I aware of language as a potential problem? I really still don't know: what I do know is that I arrived in Berkeley, in a philosophy department at the time when Anglo-Saxon universities were—to make matters worse for me—involved mainly in linguistics (and, I should add, symbolic logic). It had not occurred to me that the ten words and five sentences I could manage in English were no preparation to audit such complicated courses. I did my best; read *Time* magazine avidly, listened to jazz records, and within six months I was pretty much integrated—at least superficially—into American university life.

Something happened, though, which determined my life: I fell in love with the American language. I was thrilled by the Californian way of speaking English, by the style, the lingo, the slang, of American publications, by the "specialized" languages of American sports; listening to baseball games or football games was like entering secret worlds. I don't know if I liked the games in their own right or the whole ritualistic language that went with them. I used to feel proud of describing games, to friends, in their right terminology. I was happy to use idiomatic expressions, to understand cowboy talk and small town talk. I knew, in American, things I could not tell in any of the languages I knew, because my experiences in those languages were limited, or seemed limited, or were too familiar to keep for me a sense of discovery. Speaking in America was like going up the Amazon River, full of dangers, full of wonders.

At the University things were different. I had a hard time trying to find interest in my new studies; I had to redirect deeply rooted habits of thinking and feeling. I remember how amazed I was, or rather how shocked, when I heard that one of my fellow students, a young Yugoslav man, had the subject he proposed for his Ph.D. thesis rejected. He wanted to write on Nietzsche and they told him that this was not acceptable because Nietzsche was not a philosopher, but a poet (things have changed since the cultural revolution of the sixties and I doubt that today this subject matter would be refused on the same grounds). But I was all the more unable to understand the Department's decision, given that I considered philosophy, after Hölderlin and Heidegger, as finding its greatest expression in poetry.

I was doing very little writing those days because I was in a state of permanent discovery: a whole new world was being opened day after day, and that included the discovery of nature as a force, a haunting beauty, a matter of daylight dreaming, an obsession. Riding in a car on the American highways was like writing poetry with one's whole body. I did not stay more than a few years at the University and never wrote any doctoral thesis. I found a job in a small college in Marin County, close to San Francisco, teaching Humanities. I was happy.

I was starting something new, a new experience, and the feeling of some sort of stability, a profession which has its own rhythms, brought me back to the desire for writing. I still considered myself as a French speaking person, even if I was teaching in English. But when I thought seriously about poetry and writing again, I discovered a problem of a political nature. It was during the Algerian war of independence. The morning paper was regularly bringing news of Algerians being killed in the war, or news of the atrocities that always seem to accompany large-scale violence. I became suddenly, and rather violently, conscious that I had naturally and spontaneously taken sides, that I was emotionally a participant in the war, and I resented having to express myself in French. Today I do not have these violent reactions towards the French language because the problem has long been settled. There is peace between Algeria and France. Then, things were different: Arab destiny as a whole seemed to be dependent on the outcome of that conflict. The dream of Arab unity was very alive then, and Algeria was its symbol.

I realized that I couldn't write freely in a language that faced me with a deep conflict. I was disturbed in one fundamental realm of my life: the domain of meaningful self expression. Something quite unexpected solved my problem, a solution which was like the opening of a side window, as if one morning the sun did not rise where it was expected to rise, but close by, at a different point of the horizon. I met, on the Berkeley campus, a woman who was the head of the Art Department of the College. Her name is Ann O'Hanlon. We chatted in the middle of an alley next to rose bushes, and when I told her that one of the courses I was teaching was Philosophy of Art, she asked me if I was painting, and when I said "no," she wondered how one dealt with the philosophy of a subject one did not practice, and my answer was, I remember clearly, that my mother had told me I was clumsy. She said: "And did you believe her?!"

The fateful conversation not only instantaneously freed my hands, but also, like a planet changing orbits, it directed my attention, and then my energies, toward a new art form which meant a new universe of interests. I went to the Art Department in my free time and I started painting. I soon realized that to me this meant a new language and a solution to my dilemma: I didn't need to write in French anymore, I was going to paint in Arabic.

All this was happening around the year 1960. Furiously, I became a painter. I immersed myself in that new language. Abstract art was the equivalent of poetic expression; I didn't need to use words, but colors and lines. I didn't need to belong to a language-oriented culture but to an open form of expression (many years later, traveling in Morocco, I had a discussion with a Morroccan painter who told me that in his view Morocco has so many good painters because this is the way their best artists solve the language problem, those of the generation who grew up under the dominance of French culture). My spirit was loose. I understood that one can move in different directions, that the mind, unlike one's body, can go simultaneously in many dimensions, that I moved not on single planes but within a spherical mental world, and that what we consider to be problems can also be tensions, working in more mysterious ways than we understand. As time passed, and as I taught in English, I felt more and more at ease with this new language I was using. I was not using this new language, I was living it.

Then, there was Vietnam. America in Vietnam. Vietnam in the American psyche. The war on television. The protests in the streets. The cultural revolution that was taking place in America had Vietnam as one of its sources, and one of its consequences was that the war issue became also a literary rallying point, a concern for the poets and a dynamic subject matter. Poets wrote against the war, or rather, fought against the war through poetry.

One day—I was particularly affected by the war images on the television screen, and was tired and dispirited—I found on the table of the Professors' Lounge a literary magazine looking like a newspaper folded in four; it said it was distributed freely, and welcomed poetry as action against the war. That was the *S.-B. Gazette* (S and B standing for Sausalito and Belvedere, two elegant small towns north of San Francisco). I came home, put a piece of paper in my typewriter and, almost as if not paying attention to what I was doing, wrote a poem: "The ballad of the lonely knight in present-day America," and sent it to the *S.-B. Gazette*. In a few days came a note scribbled with a pencil on a torn notebook page saying "poem much welcome" and below: "send more!" and was signed "Leon Spiro." I was a poet in the English language!

I wrote some other poems, dictated by emotions and events, and felt part of an immense movement of American poets at a time when poetry seemed to grow in that country like music and grass. One day Robert Kennedy was asked by journalists, for maybe the tenth time in his life, how he felt about his brother's absence. Bobby

Kennedy cried and as an answer cited Romeo's speech on Juliet's beauty in the night. I was so moved to see a man, in a culture that denies men the need to cry as being a sign of weakness, cry openly for his dead brother and express through Shakespeare his sense of the inner unity of love, that I wrote to him and said I would be happy if he read the poem I had written, the first one, the ballad. I got a wonderful answer telling me he was moved by the text.

Letters arrived asking me if I would participate in poetry readings or have the poems I wrote republished in some anthologies. I received letters from poets from the United States or Latin America which were sent just to share thoughts. That was a time when poetry became, for a few years, the only religion which has no gods and dogmas, no punishments, no threats, no hidden motivations, no commercial use, no police, and no Vatican. It was an open brotherhood open to women, men, trees, and mountains.

I was entering the English language like an explorer: each word came to life, expressions were creations, adverbs were immensely immense, verbs were shooting arrows, a simple preposition like "in" and "out" an adventure! Writing was a sport, sentences were like horses, opening space in front of them with their energies, and beautiful to ride.

The old ghosts had not disappeared. The Arab World did not vanish from my preoccupations. On the contrary. I was starting to travel in the summers to Morocco, or Tunisia, or back to Jordan, Syria, Lebanon. I made friends with many Arab poets of Arabic or French expression. Poetry and painting stayed separate, but one day when I decided to write, or, to be precise, copy poetry in Arabic with the intent to integrate "calligraphy" into a style of working with watercolors and inks which was contemporary, I engaged myself on a trail that is still in front of me. I found Japanese folded papers, like the old books of Japanese woodcuts where each double page was an image tied, or not tied, to the following ones. Something from my childhood emerged: the pleasure of writing, line after line, Arabic sentences which I understood very imperfectly: I took modern poetry written by the major Arab poets and "worked" with them. I did not try to have them translated to me, I was satisfied with the strange understanding of them: bits here and there, sentences where I understood but one key word; it was like seeing through a veil, looking at an extraordinary scenery through a screen, as if the screen did not erase images but toned them down and made them look even more mysterious than they were.

Year after year I worked on these long papers, like horizontal scrolls, with my imperfect writing, aware that it was the opposite of classical calligraphy that was at stake;

it was reading through the art of a poet's work. These works have been exhibited in galleries in the United States and in some Arab capitals. They arouse questions, they provoke passionate discussions, they puzzle most of the time, they make their ways in magazines, articles, and critics' studies. They represent to me a coming to terms which I would never have expected until it happened, with the many threads that make up the tapestry of my life. I integrated myself in the cultural destiny of the Arabs by very indirect ways, and I hope that the search is not over.

Where am I now?

I gave up teaching in the early seventies and went back to Beirut. I left the United States suddenly. I came into a city which was going through its best years. I threw myself into the center of an active volcano. It was fascinating. I found myself again in a French speaking world, French and Arabic, but mostly French for me, as I found a job as director of the cultural pages of a French speaking and newly founded daily paper. It was good to again be where Arab history was seemingly happening, to go to Aleppo for a vacation instead of the Sierras, and to know more of Cairo and Damascus than of New York. It was refreshing, it was exciting, this shift into new territory. Beirut had moved so fast that it was for me a brand new city.

Of course, I wrote in French, left English aside out of necessity. I was too busy to meditate on its consequences on anything called a "literary career." Literature has never been a profession to me, it has been something for books. My own writing was like my own breathing: something I was doing.

A tragic and nasty war erupted in Beirut in 1975. People's lives exploded with the buildings and, like the pieces of the destroyed buildings, they went in all directions. Some of us went to Paris. French speaking Lebanese went to Paris. English speaking Lebanese went to London or New York. Some, mostly for business purposes, went to Arab countries. I went to Paris two years after the war had started, not to stay indefinitely but to wait for things to calm down in Lebanon. Things did not calm down, as we all know, they went from bad to worse, from civil war to occupation. When in Paris, I heard of a terrible thing that had happened in Lebanon: a woman I knew a little but respected immensely was kidnapped by Christian militiamen, tortured and killed. I am not telling her story here, only that the "reasons" for her ordeal were not morally acceptable. I wrote a book, a fiction based on reality, about this tragic incident: *Sitt Marie-Rose* was written and published in Paris. In French.

I had personal reasons, a few years later, to go back to California, as going back to Beirut looked more and more a difficult thing to do. The paper I was working for had closed. Other difficulties were to be considered.

Back in California. What would I do in California but paint and also write. I realized that I think more happily, with a more natural flow, when I don't fight my environment. I would even say that my writing is influenced, or rather grows, the way plants grow out of soil and water, from the land I am inhabiting. So whenever I write in America, I write in English.

What can I say of the fact that I do not use my native tongue and do not have the most important feeling that as a writer I should have, the feeling of a direct communication with one's audience? It is like asking what I would have been if I were somebody else. There are no answers to such questions. These questions are like trying to hold reflections in one's hands. There are a growing number of writers who use an "international" language, like English, who use in fact another language than their own because of history, or because of exile, or because of personal taste.

Do I feel exiled? Yes, I do. But it goes back so far, it lasted so long, that it became my own nature, and I can't say I suffer too often from it. There are moments when I am even happy about it. A poet is, above all, human nature at its purest. That's why a poet is as human as a cat is a cat or a cherry tree is a cherry tree. Everything else comes "after." Everything else matters, but also sometimes does not matter. Poets are deeply rooted in language and they transcend language.

Someone can stand up and ask me why didn't I, on my own, at some point in my life, learn Arabic? This is a question that sometimes haunts me. I don't go on accusing the old colonial system (like Franz Fanon so beautifully did). I am not, and Arab writers are not, for example, in the situation of the Black African writers whose native languages have been totally eradicated by both the French colonial administration and then by their own governments. Arab writers are totally responsible for the language they use.

I have always been part of the here and now. I did not take time out of everyday life to consecrate all my efforts to acquire Arabic as a full language. When the sun is strong and the sea is blue I can't close my windows and go in and "study" anything. I am a person of the perpetual present. So I stayed "outside." Arabic remained a forbidden paradise. I am both a stranger and a native to the same land, to the same mother tongue. This century told us too many times to stay alone, to cut all ties, never to look back, to go and conquer the moon: and this is what I did. This is what I do.

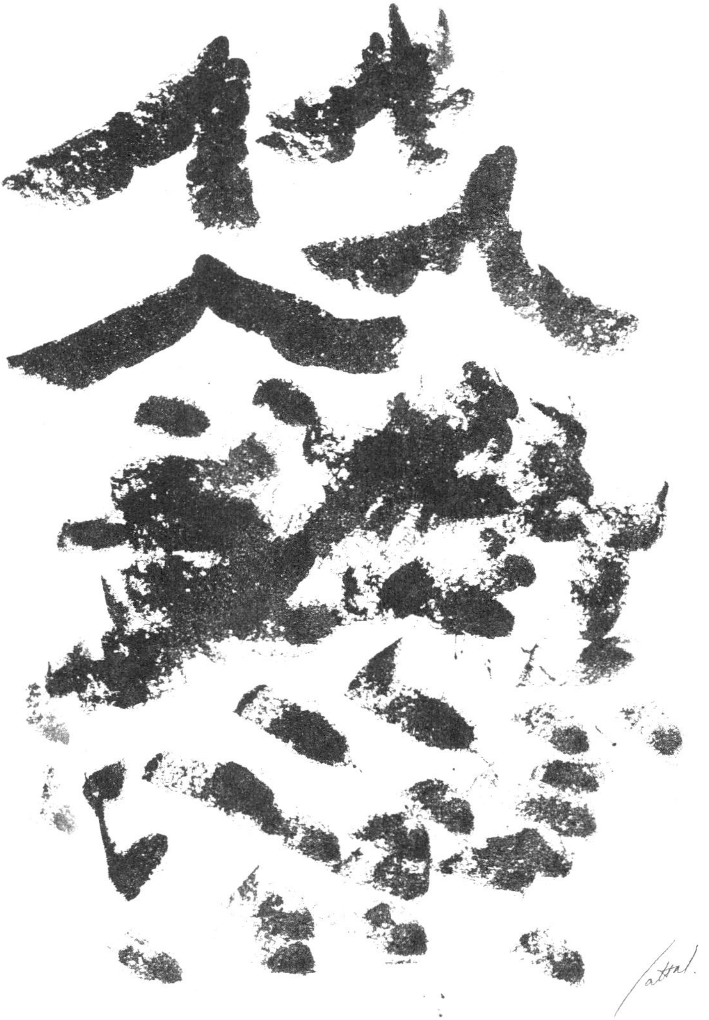

GROWING UP TO BE A WOMAN WRITER IN LEBANON (1986)

THE THING THAT I REMEMBER AS THE OLDEST my memory has retained—the first object in my private archaeology—is a circular stone fountain, low and made of what I think now was soft limestone. And that fountain was empty.

I don't know if I lived in the house which had that garden and the fountain, or if I visited it with my mother. But it is there with a singular and haunting clarity.

The house I remember very well, the one in which I see the little girl I was, was an old big house, with huge windows, lace curtains, a flower stand painted in green with ferns or other permanently green plants in pots, and a garden with a tall wall delineating its territory from the street. It was in Beirut. I remember light all over the place, I remember it to be cool, with my bed in my parents' bedroom, and a kitchen which had a door to another side of the same garden. I remember flowers as clearly as I remember my mother and her cat. Bijou was our cat and she had kittens regularly.

I was an only child and it seemed like I lived in a magic place. I liked it. I had space to run, I had places to inhabit. There were four rooms each one with a different personality, I could be a different person in each one of them. One of them was sunny and my father used to shave in it. It had sunshine. The sun was like something real coming through the windows. It had existence. It jumped off the mirrors of the tall cupboards. The bedroom was cooler. Its light was more evenly distributed along the year. The third one was well furnished but I did not often go into it. My mother used to close its door. The fourth one was useless. It had a window bearing on the living room inside. It was dark, almost black, and reserved for the cat when she had her kittens. Nobody needed that room.

I was much aware that I was a little girl. There was something nice about being a little girl, something warm and comfortable. Something electric also. I was aware that I was more like my mother than my father. But as I did not have other children around me to compare the way they were treated, I felt more like something alive, a "being," a person, than specifically a little girl. And I did not go to school until I was five.

There is related one event which stays clear in front of my eyes: we had a little boy visiting us. He was half French by his mother and his name was Pierrot. His father was a French citizen from Indo-China. The little boy was an orphan. His French mother had died in Beirut. He came to us for his vacations from boarding school. I remember that one day, very likely before noon, we were playing in the space between a couch and the wall with its windows. Pierrot offered to uncover himself if I would do the same so that we see "how we are made." So, we did take some of our clothes off, but we heard my mother moving around in the house and pulled back our clothes. That was all. I don't know if my memory is faithful. But it seems that I took the experience as something I learned, with a kind of numbness, the feel of the pure looking at something. But I did not forget. The moment remains singular and clear. And close to age sixty, I found that it had made its way into a poem I wrote recently: "An alley of linden trees, and lightning . . ." It reads:

> This is why I kept company with
> archangels and ants
> as well as with a seven-year-old
> child who since has died
> leaving no trace
> one day over the radio it was said
> that he received two bullets
> in the head
> it was in Saigon the day the war ended

I lost track of Pierrot far back in my own childhood; the

war in Vietnam happened and I put my energies into the anti-war movement, writing my first poetry in the language and the land of America, and then, sometime in 1985, writing a long poem about my earlier years, Pierrot and his Indo-Chinese origins and the Vietcong . . . all came together through the mystery, as well as into the mystery of poetry.

As I said, my parents sent me to school at the age of five. My mother was a Greek from Smyrna, and my father was a Syrian from Damascus who belonged to a family where the men served in the Army of the Ottoman Empire. He was the commander of Smyrna during the First World War, and although he was already married and the father of a boy and of two girls, he married my mother who was about twenty years younger than he was. His first family had remained in Damascus. At the end of the war he came to settle in Beirut and I was born in 1925.

Lebanon was newly created as a state by the French. They turned Syria and Lebanon into mandates under their rule. They expanded the already existing French schools in the country and favoured the establishment of new ones. They created in Lebanon, and imposed on it, a system of education totally conforming to their schools in France, an education which had nothing to do with the history and the geography of the children involved.

So at age five I started speaking French and then, only French, as Arabic was a forbidden language in these French schools. They were in their entirety run by members of the French Catholic Church. And Arabic was forbidden. The Lebanese children spoke it at home. My mother not knowing Arabic, French took over as the language at home: we spoke less and less Turkish or Greek and more and more French.

These schools were for boys or girls only. The co-educational system was instituted in Lebanon in the fifties.

The French nuns were stern. They behaved like colonialists and like missionaries: they had the dual purpose of extolling the virtues of French civilisation and the infallibility of the Church in matters of religion. They created for children an authoritarian and dogmatic environment. They were so thorough in their system that very few students ever questioned the education they received. Dogmatism has the effect of occupying the totality of one's mental space to such a degree that the things it purports to be true become as "natural" as the sky or earth: they become the only things the mind can distinguish, they become the very tools of one's thinking. They become taken for granted.

So I grew up thinking that the world was French. And that everything that mattered, that was "in books," or had authority (the nuns), did not concern our environment. This is what is called alienation.

I loved school because there I found other children to play with, and recreation time was my favourite time. We had fifteen minutes at ten in the morning and fifteen minutes at two in the afternoon. A square courtyard with a kiosk and an empty fountain in its middle was our playground, and was for me an enchanted garden that still recurs in my dreams.

I was very much aware that I was a little girl because of my mother's careful attention to my dresses: little pieces of silk cloth were going to the dressmaker to make me elaborate little dresses which were worn for special occasions and given to the "poor" in perfect condition one or two years later. I still miss them and am left with the feeling that I never wore them to the full.

One day I was caught by the nuns while climbing the fence of the courtyard: it was a low fence made of slim painted iron poles, and it was easy to press oneself on the railing and slide to the other side. But the nuns caught me and with a stern voice accused me of being a "tomboy" which in French is called *garçon manqué* ("something that failed to be a boy")! It made being a boy both appealing as a fact and shameful as a desire. One should say that with their obsession with sins—French Catholicism having a Calvinistic streak in it—the nuns did their best to spoil our natural innocence. I could say that my earlier creative works were the invented confessions of non-existent sins. The priests were always asking for more, implying that we had sins that were hidden from them; so I invented (and other children did too, I learned later) stealing candy, telling lies to my mother, hurting Jesus' feelings during mass by chatting, and having bad thoughts . . . not knowing that the priests meant sexual daydreaming by bad thoughts. So, I now consider these early fabrications as a sort of story-telling, little moments of imaginative thinking.

I was told early in my life that little girls were in "danger." My mother never let me go alone anywhere, and allowed me to go playing with friends of only two families, one on our street, the other about two blocks from our house. She used to give me counseling. It was very simple: do not go behind the counter at the grocery store, do not accept candy from strangers, stay always outside and visible. Once she said: "do not go behind the counter because the storekeeper can pull out a knife and kill you in the belly." I still shudder at the image, but I was only puzzled then, wondering why the old man with his cap down over his ears, sitting endlessly behind huge sacks of lentils and rice in his tiny store would have ever done such a thing. He barely talked to me.

The admonitions grew more serious when I was an adolescent. And when at college age I expressed the desire to go to Paris to study, my mother simply said: "There the men will devour you." She managed with a few sentences here and there to create an image of the world that I discovered later in movies like *Jack the Knife*,[1] where men are like the Chaos of Greek mythology, the original void, the unending vertigo.

Looking back at those years, I also wonder if my mother didn't suffer from the fact that I was her only child and that she didn't have a son.

It must have been the month of June, when school was out and summer was officially ushered in; was I ten or nine when she bought a piece of black satin and made a costume for me on her sewing machine: billowing and extremely short pantaloons of shining and black satin, and a white satin blouse with long sleeves? She also made a flowing black tie. She took me to the hairdresser, the neighbourhood coiffeur, whose store smelled of soap and *eau de cologne*. She asked him to cut my hair very short, "à la garçon," a hair-do I discovered later was very chic and popular in French fashion magazines of the time. My hair was cut the way Rimbaud had his hair in one of his famous pictures that one sees on the cover of editions of his poems. There was a picture of me taken that summer,

1. The film to which Adnan is likely referring is *Jack the Ripper.—Ed.*

in the family album, a precious book of photographs ranging from the First World War to the forties. That album was entrusted to an Armenian family who were friends of mine—the three sisters who had stayed in Beirut fled during the Civil War in Lebanon, and they destroyed or dispersed the things I had left with them for years. They thought they would never locate me, but it happened that I met one of them, after many years of absence, on a Beirut sidewalk the day after the destruction of the most important documents I had inherited from my parents.

Being dressed as a boy made me feel very happy. I felt special: no other girls that I knew ever dressed like that. (In fact, no boys, either). It was a dress suitable for the movies or the theater. I thought I looked beautiful in it, if not beautiful, certainly touched by some magic. In fact, it must have reinforced my identity of being neither just a girl, nor a boy, but a special being with the magical attributes of both.

In fact, my singularities accumulated. I was the only "only" child at school, the only one among the children considered "natives" by the ever-present nuns. I had met one or two girls who, like me, had neither brothers nor sisters, but they were French, and French people were expected to have few children as opposed to the large Lebanese families. It was regarded as a sign of aristocracy to be among few at home. There were also French families with ten or eleven children, but they were very "Catholic," they went to church in a row, and somehow they looked poorer, more "common." They did not fit the image of the superior and aloof French.

I was also the only child of mixed background: my father was a Muslim and my mother a Christian. Such a mixed marriage was an anomaly. It attracted attention and often mysterious remarks: there was a hushed antagonism. My mother was scorned by some for having married a Muslim. She was pitied by others: "Such a beautiful woman like you married to a Turk," some women neighbours would say. For most people my father, although an Arab, was a Turk because of his service in the Ottoman Empire. To marry a Muslim Turk was somehow worse than having married an Arab, at least in the eyes of the Maronite Christians who were more and more in positions of power in the new Lebanon. My mother took it in her stride, but once in a while she would feel guilty and, turning to a lit olive oil lamp in our bedroom and the icon, she would ask the Greek Virgin Mary, in Greek, sometimes with tears, "Oh Panaya, have I done something wrong in marrying him? Will you forgive me?!"

I absorbed that sense of guilt, or at least the sense that there was something in our family which was unique, this uniqueness being sensed by me as a privilege mixed with some shame: I felt both rebellious and apprehensive any time an allusion was made to the religious make-up of my family.

This question of religion or religions haunted my life. By the end of the kindergarten year the French nuns called in my mother and said something along these lines: "This child is six years old already and is not baptised. Do you realise that if anything happens to her she will go to limbo."

My mother must have felt ashamed that she had not resolved that question with my Muslim father. She was a Greek, a woman in a new country and a new culture, respecting authority. The sisters told her that I was asking to be baptised because I loved the little Jesus so much. My father, who was twenty years older than his wife, and also a rather defeated man, let her decide. She decided that as I was going to a French school and as the sisters were so nice as to insist and worry, they could arrange a baptismal ceremony. As children were usually baptised at birth I felt proud and very special in having in a way witnessed my own ceremony. It was in the French church of Beirut, the rite was Latin. For the sisters I was becoming practically a French child, and they were particularly fond of me for years to come. I was something they had worked for and conquered.

I was very conscious of my new privilege, but a division remained and settled in my heart. My father and I used to go very regularly to Damascus, where my aunt Fahima lived with her husband and her two sons. My father loved Damascus, the city of his own childhood, with tenderness. He was different when he was there: relaxed, mysterious, romantic. And I was happy there, in a house where Arabic and Turkish were spoken, and never French. It was another world, with Muslim feasts involving dinners on huge copper trays put on the rugs and trays of sweets brought in from the market by boys carrying them on their heads.

Damascus was the East, with its splendour, its specific qualities, its hushed conversations, its sense of history and grandeur. There I was a child of city Arabs mixed with Turkish blood and culture, of Arabs who were wondering if the Ottoman Empire was really any worse than the new colonisation. In Beirut it was worry and everyday life, in Damascus it was magic and recreation. In Beirut I was a little Christian. In Damascus I was at the door of the Islamic world.

Thus I got used to standing between situations, to being a bit marginal and still a native, to getting acquainted with notions of truth which were relative and changed like the hours of the days and the passing of seasons.

I ended up not being religious, seeing in the discourse held by the nuns some vague trap, some temptation I was refusing, some challenge to the world of my father, a father who always appeared weaker than my mother but always dignified. In my adolescence I viewed him as a tragic figure.

The world of a writer, even at its most fictional, and particularly the world of a poet, is not a pure construct of the mind. The energy that carries creative work to its expression, and the very content of creative work, comes from life experiences, and maybe even from some memories carried in our genes. I cannot separate the events that shape my day-to-day existence from whatever I write and paint.

There is a dialectical relation between one's life and one's work. The former obviously influences the latter, but one's work also becomes an influence on one's life. It is a two-way affair, a mysterious process where what we call life and what we call creation, merge and do not merge, cross-feed each other.

I loved the fact, the act, of writing, as far as I can remember. In elementary school we were given words around which to build a sentence. I used to write long paragraphs, enjoying the pen, the ink, the page, and the words coming one after another with a feel of roundness, a comfort for the body and the mind. Later, we had composition classes. We had to write a few pages on a given topic. My writings were often singled out by the teacher and read out loud in the class as a model. Once I was accused of having cheated, copied what I wrote, because the teacher could not believe that I had written the text I turned in to her. I also used to write the homework of my classmates. The pleasure of inventing little stories, of achieving a sort of triumph, of winning a sort of victory, of having kids come around me for sentences and words, while I was not best at running or at volleyball, made me feel early in life that writing was my little domain, a world where I had no fear, no tension, no problem.

I speak of writing and not of reading books because the homes in Beirut in the twenties and thirties did not have shelves of French books, of children's or adults' books in French. Some had no bookshelves at all. Books were rare, considered expensive, and in the libraries of scholars. What was called an average home had just a few, usually some religious or poetic works in Arabic. My parents, each having been uprooted many times, had at home my father's Quran, my mother's book of the Gospels in Greek, a Turkish-German dictionary from my father's War College days in Istanbul, and a few novels in Greek about Cleopatra, Egyptian Saints of the Desert, and love stories . . . books my mother at some time in her life read aloud to her niece who came to live with us for a while.

So I was more interested in writing than in reading, a pattern which fitted the other patterns of my existence: as an only child I had to invent my games, imaginary game companions, and my stories. This must have been true to such a point that I remember in pre-kindergarten times the mirrors of the cupboards, in which I was looking, and imagining that the little child I was seeing, which was myself, was a little friend of mine who came to visit.

The years that qualify most as being a writer's or poet's formative years are the years of our adolescence. These are years when our reason and our senses grow conspicuously, but in separate ways, and develop as if independently from one another. This is why they are years of violent emotions and mental confusion. We are then like some young trees whose branches grow in different directions giving the impression that the stem will break apart under opposite pulls.

A young girl in Beirut in the late thirties was seen as an endangered species to be protected from future predators. Mothers were sentimental about them, looking into the not-so-far future where a young man would appear on the horizon and marry their daughters. A little girl was a daughter, a school girl, and a future wife. She was never considered as an autonomous being whose life could turn out to be something other than what was dictated to be the social norm.

Rape was never discussed socially and never mentioned in the newspapers or in classrooms, but mothers thought about it all the time and made sure that their daughters were not playing in courtyards, gardens, or the streets, with boys who were friends of their sons. The division of the world between a masculine universe and a feminine universe was established by the time children were seven years old, what the Catholic church called the age of reason, a division which also exists in the Islamic world.

Not having a brother at home, I did not see boys of my age until I went to college. I was in girls' schools, visited with my mother's families where only little girls sat with us. But I went to the movies at an early age, early enough so that the sisters called in my mother and told her that my imagination was running wild because I was going to the movies. There was indeed a fire in the house! Movies were then mostly for adults, and the kids I went to school with were marveling at the fact that my parents allowed me to watch them. Maybe because I was an only child and it was normal for my parents to take me with them wherever they went—my father to Damascus, my mother on visits and to the movies.

My image of men, of love, of interaction with the outside world, the world at large, was formed uniquely by the cinema of the thirties and the early forties. And that cinema was not local, it was the cinema of Hollywood and France. I used to go to the movies and come out of them with a fever. My head was turning and my heart beating. I developed a secret life inhabited by men and women who looked infinitely more attractive than the saints whose lives were tediously explained to us during religious studies. At age ten I was already in love with Marlene Dietrich, Greta Garbo, and Gary Cooper while I was falling in love with the little girl sitting next to me in school. My first passion. A love which manifested itself by running and playing catch in recreation time, by holding my breath when that little being looked at me, and by exchanging stamps. My father had a collection of stamps going back to the end of the nineteenth century. I gave it all to that little girl. It was only two or three years later that my father discovered the disappearance of his collection. He asked me if I had taken it and I think I said, yes, and that I had given them all away. He shook his head taking it, I am sure, as one more defeat in his life, and never said another word about the matter.

The movies provided me with the occasion for having a parallel life outside the gaze of my mother: the thing I remember as the hardest about my childhood, the hardest to live with, was the fact that we had no life of our own, no privacy, neither physical nor moral. People in the Arab world, and certainly elsewhere in the Third World, are never really left alone, they live under the scrutiny of everybody around. This is also true of Greece, Italy and Spain, at least in the popular strata of their societies.

Developing private thoughts was my first rebellion, my first emancipation. Private life came much later. So I am accustomed to equating freedom with thinking, and I was made ready to understand political rebellion as an affirmation of the self.

By the time I reached fourteen, a new problem faced me at home: studying in a language basically foreign to my parents created a distance between us. I was engaging my life in territories alien to them and I was being estranged. I felt more and more different, with frames of reference they could not share. I was becoming a foreigner in my own house.

My father respected learning to such a point that he didn't interfere with matters of education. He must have known that there was no use fighting an unavoidable national situation. He was too much of a military man not to understand that military defeats carry with them a multitude of consequences, which affect every aspect of life. My mother viewed the world in rather simple ways. All she saw was that I was growing to be different from her and it must have increased her loneliness and her sense of exile. At that time I could not understand what was going on. I only knew that I was subjected to tensions which gradually evolved into hostility: I started hating her because her views, her authority, and what must have been her desperation, were becoming unbearable to me. She began hating the very education she was striving to give me at school. She was hating the books, and my friends, and was starting to harass me by putting out the lights when I was reading or obliging me to go to bed early to make sure I would not sink into some book or magazine that she viewed as enemies and intruders.

By the time I was fifteen, the Second World War was in full operation and I was taken out of school. My mother declared that prices had gone up enormously and that we were too broke for the family to afford a private school, public schools being practically non-existent in Beirut. But things were not as simple as I was made to believe they were. I must say here that a few years before I interrupted school my mother had taken charge of a little boy, the son of her niece who used to come to visit us. That young woman had fallen in love and was expecting a child. She was not married and she panicked. My mother convinced her to keep the child and promised to take care of him. She assumed his upbringing.

By the time I was sixteen, the war was on, the presence of

the French army in Lebanon increased, and the French, in their war effort with their English allies, needed local help. Beirut became a boom town. Offices multiplied. Young girls were finding jobs as secretaries both in the military and in the civilian sectors of the war economy. The first generation of Arab girls going to work in offices with men was being born. Inflation and job opportunities made families accept that their girls should work. This new way of life shook society and a little revolution took place, a social revolution, that went unnoticed. Girls were still required to come home just after work, but you could see them steal away for a few hours that they spent with boyfriends in the coffee shops and the tea houses that mushroomed in Beirut overnight and as if by enchantment.

In that city, exploding socially, but in subtle ways, in ways nobody talked about, everybody behaved as if life hadn't changed. My mother decided that I should take a job she found in the French Information Bureau, a job consisting at first of filing papers and receiving the mail that the postmen, or the British soldiers called dispatch carriers, were regularly bringing in large leather pouches hung over their motorcycles. It was the beginning of adventure. And it happened inadvertently. I was in the midst of exciting hours, history was being made practically before my eyes. I was following on maps, with French and British officers and officials, the advance and the retreat of armies. Black pins for the Germans, red pins for the Russians, blue pins for the Allied Forces were moving day to day like the soldiers they represented.

I gained the confidence of the administrator of the Bureau I was working for, and although my pay was the lowest, maybe just ahead of the office boys', I started to type and sometimes answer letters on my own. The news was formulated in the office and distributed to the daily papers. I witnessed how political influence was wielded and how much propaganda was part of warfare. I had no theories, I had not the means to draw large-scale conclusions, I had no political upbringing, no college training, but I was watching events in their rawness, I was participating in my own limited ways in a cosmic adventure. The magic of these years still haunts me. It is of such stuff that literature is made, even in the most indirect of ways.

Something though was eating me: the sense of having left school too early, of something left unfinished, of a world which held its own fascination for me and of which I was kept out. One October morning (classes in Lebanon start in the early days of October), I was crying in the office, and the "boss," a writer and former teacher, saw my tears and called me to his office to find out the reason for my sorrow. I told him that it was the first day of school, that I had left my studies for three years, and that I was desperate. He asked me not to worry and told me he would see what he could do about it. I had nothing in mind, not knowing that it was even possible that something could be done.

Jean Gaulmier, who later pursued his academic career at the Sorbonne, in Paris, then arranged my office hours in such a way that I was free in the morning till eleven. In exchange I had to work an evening schedule, leaving the office at eight or nine, the chauffeur of the office being charged to drive me home. These were war years, there was sometimes a curfew, and it was out of the question that young ladies walk alone at night in the streets of the city.

My life changed again. I enrolled for the French baccalaureate, a degree which is given in two terms, and is roughly the equivalent of a junior college degree. I skipped a whole year of studies, by special permission, and I went to the morning classes considered the most important for the exam. The other studies I managed with a series of tutorial courses, some on Sundays, some during school vacations.

I passed the first part with high honours as well as the second part. I was the only person who had ever passed these two exams without going regularly to classes and, also, while working full time at an exciting and demanding job. The baccalaureate is a state examination and, after the completion of its second part, a student is automatically entitled to enter the university of his or her choice.

I certainly was happy, aware that I was leading a double or triple life: I was living in three unconnected worlds, the one at home losing its grip on me. But I was losing contact with my parents: I was home only to sleep at night, and years later I realised how their hearts were being broken. My father was aging rapidly, my mother too, and home was not a happy and exciting place anymore. With the cruelty of adolescence I had only one dream: to get away from it as quickly as possible. My parents sensed it and they must have felt betrayed and abandoned.

I have said earlier that as a child I used to love to write. The act of writing, the alignment of sentences, the warm impact of words, the excitement of learning new ones through the subjects we studied, geography words, history words, chemistry words, all that was the discovery of an invisible world made sometimes more real than my bedroom or the streets of Beirut.

By the time I was nineteen and eligible for the university, I thought that I liked mathematics above all, and architecture. There was no school of architecture, then, in Lebanon, and it was the engineering school that was licensing the builders. I declared one day at home that I wanted to become an engineer: it created one more scandal. My mother was horrified as if confirmed in her belief that I was veering from the norm. She said that that was a profession for men, and she said it in a way that carried the intention to shame. There was something immoral in my demands and she said that even if I asked for a scholarship to pay for my studies she would not let me leave the office. "We need the money," she said. And when I remarked that her little nephew was costing her a lot of money for his schooling, she replied that he was a boy and that men deserved any sacrifice made for their education. So I could not go any further on that matter. I knew that I had no recourse.

It happened then that the French University was opening a branch in literature: an autonomous institute for literature and linguistics named École Supérieure des Lettres de Beyrouth. The enrollment fees were minimal, and, most importantly in my case, the classes were scheduled for the afternoon or early evenings. By then the war was over, the war bureaus were closed, and I found a day-time job that allowed me both to bring money home and to be free to go to class again.

The École des Lettres was founded by an exceptional Frenchman who was for years the chief administrator of all the French schools in Lebanon and Syria. He was an appointee of the French Ministry for Foreign Affairs and had the prestige and the power of a top diplomat. It happened, we learned, that he disliked the control of the French University in Beirut by the Jesuits and wanted to create a separate Institute for literature, linguistics, and philosophy, a place for learning where ideas would not be directed toward a religious ideology. Gabriel Bounoure was his name. He was an essayist and a major critic of French literature, sending papers on literature and poetry to the prestigious literary magazine called the *NRF*. He became, in addition to his official government functions, the director of the École des Lettres and gathered in Beirut a small but exceptional staff of professors. He gave a few classes, scheduled at odd times, during vacations, or at the hours he was free from his office. I was one of the ten or twelve first students of the École. Gabriel Bounoure's classes were the equivalent of these mystic encounters one reads about either in the great Sufis' writings of the Islamic past, or in the works of German Romantic writers such as Novalis or Herman Hesse. These were not ordinary academic teachings, but rather initiations into the life of the spirit as exemplified by the works of Pascal and Descartes or the poems of Baudelaire, Gérard de Nerval, and Rimbaud. I entered literature by the grand door, I discovered the "golden rule" of the mind. I participated for three or four years in an experiment that Plato himself would have envied.

This is where and when I convinced myself that poetry was the purpose of life, poetry as a counter-profession, as an expression of personal and mental freedom, as perpetual rebellion. Poetry became a revolution, and a permanent voyage. With a few friends I felt I was living a parallel life, a life which cut all ties with home and country. I can say that I experienced the feeling of knowing what angels could be. The city itself changed in my imagination. It became an enchanted small town, orange trees perfuming some of its streets, movies and music becoming one with my thoughts. I was living at home but not seeing my parents anymore, or seeing them as through a fog. I think that is what is meant by being enraptured.

Gabriel Bounoure treated us as privileged children of Enlightenment. There was an equality in fervour, a fullness. Body and soul were one. Rimbaud and Baudelaire became more familiar to us than anybody we knew or could know. They took residence in Beirut. Along with Rilke. And Gérard de Nerval, who had written in the late nineteenth century a *Voyage to the Orient*, came back resuscitated among us. Gabriel Bounoure called him Gérard, and Gérard was one of us. The ten or twelve students of the École des Lettres became thirty or forty in a few years, but they did not dilute the intensity of the first years, rather they caught the fever, joined the paradise.

Of course the world view I had during the École des Lettres years had nothing to do with the problems of day-to-day living that people have to face. It was a view suited for pure spirits. My mother was getting scared about my future. She was eager to have me married, to see me settling into situations which were familiar to her. The tensions at home were becoming unbearable. My father was totally out of the picture: he was too old and too ill.

When I said that I wasn't interested in getting married I was accused of preferring to be adventurous and irresponsible. Sometimes I was made to understand that I was in danger of losing my mind.

One thing was true, that I realised much later: I had no idea how to run my life materially. My jobs were getting menial and badly paid.

I cannot say that I then contemplated a literary career. I did not see myself as a writer, not even a poet, but rather a person for whom poetry and the poetic life were the only concern. There were no literary magazines in French in the city, so I never thought of publishing. I did not know how one achieved success in the literary world. I do not regret it; all my life I kept the notion of poetry and literature being fragile, personal, needing distance and silence around them.

One day I wrote a paper for class. I thought it was a good paper. Somehow I was late in turning it in and I think Gabriel Bounoure represented such a figure that I was hesitant to give him my first piece of writing, the one assigned by him for his class. A friend of mine, a young man who was also a student at the École des Lettres asked to read it. He read it and liked it and decided that he would give it to his best friend who was the editor of the newspaper *Le Jour*, a daily paper in French which had a regular literary page. His friend loved the piece and published it. It was my first publication, a piece of writing on the nineteenth-century French writer, traveler, and painter, Eugène Fromentin.

So Gabriel Bounoure did not find my paper among the other papers of the class, but read it one morning in the newspaper laid on his desk. He called me in through his secretary and congratulated me. He said I had an exceptional literary sense and asked me why I had not asked for a French government scholarship to study at the Sorbonne in Paris. I said I was an only child and that my mother was difficult, and that I couldn't face her with such a decision. He said: why don't you ask her to come and see me. He thought he could convince her to let me go.

When I told my mother that Monsieur Bounoure wanted to talk to her about sending me to Paris she got pale and nervous and started to shake. She said he was an immoral man stirring us up and separating us from our families. Then she added that she had a doctor friend who kept hand grenades in his apartment against potential burglars and assassins. She threatened to go and ask for one of these weapons and come and blow up the school. The next day I warned the private secretary of Monsieur Bounoure of the dangers of my mother's visit. He laughed it off. But I was dead serious and vaguely scared for a while.

The idea of going to Paris stuck in my mind. I knew that it was going to be a matter of time before I went to the prestigious city. After all, since childhood, we were brought up to consider France the centre of the world, if not the world itself. My best friend, Lydia, a Russian girl whose parents emigrated because of the Revolution, a girl who was also the only child of her family, a few years older than me, and a being I equated with angels and spirits because she lived in an air even more rarefied than mine, had already left for Paris. Lydia had introduced me to Rilke and Gauguin (through reproductions). And to classical music. Now she had preceded me to the source of our dreams.

It seemed to me, then, that Paris was a mythical place where Rimbaud and Verlaine still quarreled in cafés. I thought that every Parisian was a poet. My mother's image of Paris was no less absolute: for her Paris was hell itself, the capital of white female slavery, the chaos in which children who have left home disappear forever. We obviously lived in irreconcilable worlds.

In 1947, my father died. The house looked empty. Something was gone forever. Then Lydia also was gone. The war with its excitement (Beiruit did not see the disasters of war, then, but only its romantic side) was a thing of the past. At a tea party, in the home of some family friends, I met an old gentleman who was a biology teacher who said that he taught in a school that was looking for a French teacher. I took the job a few weeks later. I taught French literature in a high school which was unique of its kind. Al-Ahliya School for Girls was run by a headmistress who was a Lebanese Protestant, a woman I knew closely for the two years I stayed in her school. She was an admirable person, had gone to the American University of Beirut and had a Ph.D. in Education from a university in the United States. It was my first contact with teaching and with the Anglo-Saxon oriented milieu of Lebanon.

I had no idea what I was going to do in my life. I lived from day to day. My greatest passion was for the sea. I had swum from the age of five, and very few girls of my generation were allowed to swim. There were mainly European children who were lying on the beaches. I loved the sea not only for the pleasure of swimming, but for herself. Her colours and her movements used to hypnotise me. I started one day writing a poem about her which became a long poem that I called "Le Livre de la Mer," "The Book of the Sea." It is a poem about the sea and about the sun and about their cosmic marriage. The only marriage I could care about.

At the end of 1949, I accepted the scholarship for studies in France that I was offered two years earlier. The École des Lettres was not yet staffed enough to provide all the courses needed for a university degree. I had to finish the *licence ès lettres* in France. My mother was shattered. I could not ask her for much. I was disinherited, and I felt cruel and alone. But in October I was on the plane with a few clothes and the poem on the sea still unfinished in my valise. I had a very long way to go.

VOYAGE, WAR, EXILE
(1994)

I ORIGINATED IN A PART OF THE WORLD THAT WAR has made and unmade since the beginning of this century. My memory as well as my daily life are woven with war. I often wondered how as fragile a system as the human body could bear upheavals become chronic as the ones that the Arab East has known and is still experiencing.

I was the only child of a family which has known war and exile as a consequence of war. My father was a Syrian, a high ranking officer of the Ottoman Empire, and my mother was a Greek from Smyrna, her father being a wood-carver; they met and married during World War I. In 1922, Smyrna burned in a cataclysmic fire, the war was lost, the Empire dismembered, so they came to Lebanon and settled in Beirut, a garden city with a view from all over, on the sea they knew and the most beautiful harbor of the Mediterranean.

They exiled themselves into charm and beauty. Geographically it was a bearable exile for my father, for after all, he was on Arab Land and close to his birthplace, Damascus. But he was living another exile, a terrible one this one: the empire that he knew and served had disappeared; he was living on enemy territory, a country under French occupation. I lived since my childhood with a knowledge which remained inscribed in me: that geographical exile is but the frame for an exile which goes much deeper and against which one can do nothing. As for my mother, she thought of Smyrna day and night, suffering from its absence, and often, I would say too often, I saw her questioning the horizon which encircles Beirut and wondering where Smyrna would have been, behind which cloud, on which side of the North of the setting sun. Her education had been left to hazard and to the meanderings of her life, and she resided in the twilight zone where most people live and in which they orient themselves according to their desires and sorrows.

A little after I turned twenty, I started considering going to Paris for studies in Philosophy. Considering was a term which can hardly describe my state of mind. I was impatient, yearning to go, and I did get there. My father had already died and my mother was left behind by me, with a pain whose scope I realized only much later. The amplitude of her sorrow took years to reach me. I was a bird then who flew out of her cage and was desirous to go further away. Everywhere and nowhere. Going to the cafe in those years was already a voyage and that is still one of my favorite trips.

But I went beyond the cafe. After Paris, I went to California by a series of occurrences which I am not going to linger on today. I landed in Berkeley, far, very far, from every point of view, from Beirut and from everything I knew.

This break which proved to be a radical one, was not an exile. It was adventure. I had decided to give myself a destiny for which nothing had prepared me. After a few years of study at U.C. Berkeley and Harvard I found a teaching job at a small college near San Francisco, and gave up my preparations for a Ph.D. (I should say, most happily!) It was in 1958 and I considered that I had found a roof, a salary, a reason to be, some kind of a new identity. Then followed the Sixties and the world-wide cultural revolution that they brought about. I remember this as a period where I became intensely American, and intensely an Arab, given the new perspective I acquired, from the Bay Area, on the Arab World. Most of all I sensed an exhilarating belonging to the world *per se*. I was not living an exile but a freedom which I found on my own and at my own risks. It was fun!

But we know that the Earth contains under its crust formidable plates which move constantly and in contradictory directions, creating earthquakes, and like herself, I was creating, within my soul, opposite currents equally ominous: I was espousing the dreams of the Arabs, their dramatic dreams of freedom, dignity, and unity, all symbolized then by Gamal Abdel Nasser; at the same time, and in another direction, I was plunging wholeheartedly into America, its history, its literature (falling in lasting love with the American Indians and with jazz music), aware and practically hypnotized by its frightful possibilities of mass destruction and by its incredible conquests of the moon and of space. I was living in a new time and space scale, in the absolute sense of the present, merging my own mythical time with America's own. Following the Apollo missions and its rockets, I was extra-territorial and tuned to the universe.

But the foreseeable earthquake did manifest itself; war broke out in 1967, involving Egypt, Syria, and Jordan, and America did decisively participate in the destruction of the Arabs, of their dreams and their lands, and I experienced terror, a terror that my surroundings were not sharing, and I started losing ground, getting not confused, but wounded, isolated, detached although still attached, a conflict which later made me ill for practically a whole year, from 1971 to 1972. I felt the urge to break away, go back to Beirut without looking behind me and not knowing what the future would be. I had come full circle. In the summer of '72, I was returning to Beirut literally on a stretcher. I had left as a voyager and I was coming back in exile.

I had no family left in Beirut by that summer of '72. On my father's side, my half-sisters and brother were living in Damascus. My mother's own brothers and sister had been dispersed after the fire of Smyrna in different places such as Cyprus, Alexandria, Saloniki and Genova. But it was home, after all, the more so that I was thinking that I was coming back "for good." I found a tiny apartment with a great view, five stories to climb with steep stairs, and no telephone. I could barely walk then, and I had to rebuild myself, physically and morally, while looking for a job. I reconnected with childhood friends and those I had made during the few trips that I took to Beirut during the regular summer vacations of my teaching years.

A new paper in the French language was being launched and I was hired as the editor of its cultural daily pages. The personnel was made of mostly young women or men whose enthusiasm was contagious. There was excitement in the air and these young people had the impression that they were participating in the creation of a new world, a better one, where Arabs will recover their rights and cease to be excluded from the decisions which concerned them the most.

I was both sharing the feelings of this new generation

and expecting the worst. Beirut was a laboratory and a stirring volcano. I had, after all, after Black September of 1970 and after Nasser's death, written a long poem on Beirut, the "Beirut Hell Express," which was announcing Beirut's total destruction. Of course, one does not follow one's visionary knowledge, but rather gives in to one's most obscure wishes and desires.

War did break out again, the civil war which started in April 1975. It was as if a galaxy of fire and death had been born and had started to churn with no end in sight. Like all galaxies it fed on its own energy to its bitter end. A real exodus followed: first a trickle, then a gradual and constant flow. The Lebanese started to leave. The buildings were disappearing too, the neighborhoods, the streets. With every wall which was falling and every man dying, something of a collective life and memory was being obliterated.

I was discovering—living—exile's profound meaning. What is exile if not the violent and involuntary loss of all the living symbols of one's identity? At this point, instead of me leaving, it was Beirut which was leaving me, and, we know it now, forever. Here was an exile which was total, absolute: I was in Beirut and I was witnessing that she was never going to grow normally, to remain the core of what she was. I was seeing (without any exaggeration) the meaning of Paradise lost.

Exile is a dispossession with no recourse. It is always accompanied by a feeling of humiliation: it is the "other," somebody or something, who takes possession of what you give up, or leave behind. It makes you feel pushed aside, as if you were a material object that is to be displaced.

The different forms of exile created by the Lebanese Civil War exacerbated my awareness of the conditions under which exiled people, and sometimes whole nations, live. Are not also to be considered as exiles not only people displaced from their native lands, but those who live under diverse forms of oppression, this oppression coming from foreign occupation or from their own governments?

I had seen, over and over again, with my own eyes and on television, these faces, Palestinian faces, people forced to abandon their country and who are parked into camps, or lived as foreigners on their own territory, denied the power to run their own affairs, which is to say exiled from their own selfhood. And this is true today of the Muslim Bosnians, as it is true of the Indians of the Americas, the United States included, where among other indignities, they are forbidden to study in their own schools their own languages and cultures, and practice their own religious rites. To be exiled on one's own homeland and from one's culture is maybe the most desperate of all forms of exile. It is living hell.

On these matters, where do I stand?

From the days when I was a restless (unbearably so for my parents) child, I am and have been on the move. I always loved to be on the go. I needed it and still do. Even with chronic back pain due to back operations, I moved around, and from one country to another, with no money in the bank, either, at least for most of the time. So my going to Paris or to America (as well as to Mexico, Greece, the Arab countries, etc . . .), was proceeding from inner causes the sum of which I called my free will. I didn't think of exile for the greatest part of my life. Then, what happened?

A resident, then a citizen of America, my life in California was not perceived by me as an exile but as an open-ended provisional situation. I have a passion for California. I spent in it some of the best years of my life, as well it is linked to some of the real personal tragedies that I had to go through. Then what?

The destruction of Beirut acted on me (and on so many others) as a revelatory factor. I spent the first three or four years of the war in that city (with occasional excursions abroad), and then decided to return to California, to resettle, so to speak. The break, anyhow, had never been complete. But this time I felt *obliged* to do so. It is in that way that I felt to be exiled. Thus, Beirut's destruction did force me to move but also brought a sharp light on the whole of my life.

I started looking back, thinking more and more about my parent's life, what their exile must have meant to them. I got engulfed in the desire to understand them, at last. I started counting their years, realizing things that never had occurred to me: when was my father born, I asked myself, seriously? The family papers, the old photographs, had disappeared because of the war, and little was left. The answer to my father's birth year was 1880. At last I knew for sure, and that meant that at the end of World War I, he was only 38 years old, a man defeated, his military career a thing of the past, and who never adapted to the jobs he was trying to find and to hold. As for my mother, she was only 20 when the man she had married at age 16, as the Commander of Smyrna, was destined to be poor and with his best years already behind him. A few years later they left Smyrna for good, never to return. The end of the Empire was also the end of the best (short) part of their lives.

One exile calls to the mind another kind of exile which it intensifies, defines. It is thus that in lieu of coming at last to terms with colonialism, I am more and more violently angry at it and at its consequences.

Once things get wrong, all that follows gets wrong too. For a man like my father who fought the French and the Allies in World War I, it turned out to be impossible to find a decent job in French-occupied Lebanon (or Syria, as a matter of fact). The French put into power people, mostly Maronites, who were favorable to their presence. He was therefore marginalized like so many Arab nationalists living under French or British rule.

I was born when, I suppose, my parents had already understood that their new lives were, and were to continue to be, to say the least, very limited. I had a happy childhood, though, impervious to a very large degree to their difficulties.

A new problem manifested itself, something that I perceived to be a problem only many decades later: I went to school.

At the end of World War I and following its occupation of Syria and Lebanon, the French administration installed in these countries an educational system entirely dominated by the French language and French curricula and trusted entirely to Christian schools, which depended and still depend on the French government's Ministry of Foreign Affairs. The Jesuits and the Christian brothers taught the boys, and the girls went to schools run by diverse orders of nuns. All the teachers were French missionaries at the service of both the Church and colonialism. As there was not an alternative system of education (and one large enough to absorb even a fraction of the children of schooling age), people were happy to send the children to these colonial schools. The children of my generation, those of the early thirties, received an exclusively French education. We were punished for speaking Arabic, even at recreation time. All the textbooks were imported from France and all our references, our mental tools, were becoming French. This famous "francophonie" which is so praised actually in the former French colonies was, and still is, a political tool, a factor of colonisation and alienation. We have been (like in Algeria and in Black Africa) separated from our cultural past, *exiled* from our essential language, and by way of consequence, from the history of our parents and ancestors, and projected into a mental world totally alien to our environment. We didn't have to leave our country physically, but just the same, we had left it in its most meaningful dimensions. It was even worse: given the human tendency to think that what one doesn't know doesn't therefore exist, we were led by these teachers to believe that we were being civilized because we were learning French and that there was nothing in Arabic worthy of knowing. Young and impressionable, we felt superior to the sections of the population who did not share our education. In this kind of an exile the prisoner of the new system loves his or her guardian, the victim loves its conqueror.

So, gradually, imperceptibly at first, I was being alienated from my parents: everything I knew they didn't, everything they represented was becoming strange and remote. We were raised by the schools to be cultural bastards, to yearn for France, and go!

The tragedy of education in Lebanon was not in the fact that one was learning French but in the fact that this foreign language was taught not as a second language but as a *first* language and a language superior to the native Arabic. This created political attitudes which, in my view, contributed to the confusion which fed the Lebanese Civil Var.

My recent visits to Lebanon are not encouraging on that score: given the massive destruction by the war of the school buildings, mostly public school buildings, and the paucity of the Lebanese government's budget, the French schools are taking over and pushing toward a system of education where French is favored in relation to Arabic, the balance is being lost once again, and a "grateful" citizenry is rushing to enroll its children into schools which minimize, more and more openly and arrogantly, the place of Arabic in their midst. This profound alienation that is being recreated in the aftermath of the Lebanese disaster leaves the public indifferent, or rather, unaware. Tired of controversy, people accept with no questioning whatever seems to be, at face value, a good deal . . . unfortunately.

War is a cataclysmic event which shakes the psyche and brings to the fore of consciousness ideas and emotions one thought resolved or forgotten. Memory gets heightened, overheated, so to say, thrown into a state of urgency. One's life can be put into question, forcefully, new light shed on old beliefs.

At the beginning of 1975 I was living in relative moral and intellectual comfort. I was at peace with America and at peace with the Arab world. I had a sense that problems were going to be solved, slowly but surely, both personal and national. The catastrophes that I had predicted in my own writings were denied, pushed back from my immediate attention. Lebanon was a happy place to be in.

Not that the people living in Lebanon did not have their private tragedies. The country was full of refugees, of officially recognized exiles, of refugees' camps, of close to 400,000 Palestinians who were (and still are) forbidden to go back to their original towns and villages, to whom one had to add the numerous political refugees from all over the Arab world who had come to Beirut to breathe an air of freedom and shelter their dreams.

In spite of such an overwhelming presence of people and groups of people in dire exile, I was not insisting (nor were most others) on the psychological aspects of their plight because there was such an excitement in Beirut, such a confidence in the future, such an enormous amount of political activities, that we were caught more in the romanticism of revolution than in its harsh realities. Not even the most ardent sympathizer of the Palestinians and their cause really knew what it meant to be a Palestinian refugee in Lebanon (or elsewhere). We were citizens in our own country and they were at best guests, and at worst, enemies; we had passports and could travel, they were paperless, prisoners of their condition, no-people in the eyes of the world, and this not for one or two years but for ten, twenty, thirty years . . . which meant some of them were born and raised and started growing old without ever having moved outside their camp, without knowing if they had a future . . . we didn't know what it meant for some, or most of them to listen, and having been listening to the radio on the hour by the hour for ten, fifteen, or thirty years, without hearing one good piece of news, one possibility of ever going to their home . . . that kind of an exile, we didn't know even if we were living one mile away from it, next door to it, and we had to read some of Mahmoud Darwish's poems to get a glimpse of it . . . Lebanon was in fact, for at least half the population living on its soil, made up of exiles: the Armenian refugees from World War I, the Russian refugees from that same war, Greek refugees from Smyrna, Egyptian refugees from the nationalisations of the Nasser era, all the political exiles from Syria, Iraq, Libya . . .

the Palestinians of 1948, those of 1967 . . . Still, there was a denial of all the accumulation of these anguishing situations until the whole thing, as we saw it, blew up and surprised every one and the whole world.

The war in Lebanon created in me great bitterness (and in many, of course). I found it useless from the start, cruel in its very premises. It killed a beautiful country, and what was the most extraordinary city of the 20th century: Beirut. Whatever its reasons, it could have been avoided if the will to avoid it were there. Such catastrophe, for what? That constatation makes one bitter and bitterness creates loneliness. Bitterness takes you back, creates distance between you and the other, between you and history. It therefore gives rise to a deep sense of exile, an almost metaphysical sense of exile. But exile does not kill passion. To the contrary. It enhances it but makes it utterly desperate.

Somewhere, from the middle of these long fifteen years of unending war, I entered a zone of frightful clarity.

I placed Beirut and Lebanon even more than I used to, at the center of an apocalyptic vision of the Arab world, which, by the way, I expressed later in a book-length poem which I titled "The Arab Apocalypse."

The destruction of the Arabs was decided by the Western

Powers a little after the beginning of this century, with the various treatises which followed the first world war. From the betrayal of Fayçal by the British and the French, the partitions, colonisations, political assassinations and all, we entered a destiny of doom which was mapped for us outside our will. Exile became the existential and metaphysical condition for every Arab, he being in his own country or elsewhere. It is as if one had to go further back in history or mythology, back to Hajer and Ismail, Abraham's first wife and first son, the mythical founder of the Arabian tribes, a son, a disinherited, a mother, forced into wandering and exile. But following this real/mythical past, this tragic origin, we can see that the Arab today lives as if pushed aside from his due, removed from the center of decision-making over his own future. In that sense one can affirm that the Arab is in the present world cut off from himself. When we look closely at the devastating destruction of the Arab world: Palestine, Lebanon, Algeria, Iraq eradicated physically and totally, the Sudan in havoc and Egypt threatened from the inside, and all the humiliations that the western media and politicians feel free to heap on the Arabs, we can say, to parallel Descartes' famous philosophical statement: "I think, therefore I am," that for the Arab, the existential statement that defines him would be: "I am not, therefore I am." Exile is the awareness of this marginalization and irreparable loss.

And exile is not any loss. It is irretrievable loss. It is the loss of what is closest to one's identity, the one tied to history and geography; and Arabs have been profoundly wounded in both.

And how, we can ask, does all this translate in individual terms?

Exile is a complex experience. Sometimes one falls in love with the country in which one has been forced to live. The human heart and mind are not monolithic; quite often they follow unpredictable courses. Again Mahmoud Darwish comes to one's memory. He passionately expressed his love for Beirut. The city had become his second home, his private legend, and again he had to leave, a second-time refugee, a tree twice uprooted, very likely unable to make new roots and condemned to longing and pain. People in his situation are denied ordinary happiness. They can find here and there exaltation in their work but they will never have the casual taste for living that ordinary people can enjoy, in continuity, in familiarity with their land.

Exiled people usually function on multiple tracks: they could be adapted to their new surroundings and in the same time live a life made of memories, of hidden landscapes, of double and triple allegiances, all of them honest, but excruciatingly painful when conflicts arise between the country of adoption and the old motherland. Sometimes the tensions become unbearable and people sink in depression or commit suicide. I think of so many individuals, or whole communities who, looked at from the outside, seem to lead "normal" lives but who, in the meantime, inhabit a private, imagined, paradise, forbidden and close, in which they roam like ghosts of another age. We call them "survivors," refugees, some are successful and others not, some are treated as outcasts, "terrorists," unwanted "foreigners," waiting for some final solution to their predicament, a solution which most of the time means deterioration or death.

Anyway, all along the years, I observed in exiles a special phenomenon, a syndrome, a chronic condition: to be exiled is to be defeated, and people in this case (contrary to the immigrants, for example) carry a sense of failure which rules their actions. Something in themselves seems to say that it's useless to try to beat the odds, so to speak, that failure is part of the tissue of their very being. That deep-seated feeling, so often unconscious, is a hindrance, a factor for further defeat. Exiles tend to hide, stay as anonymous as possible, as if marked by a dark star, and when they have no support group, no larger community in which to find hope and sustenance, they seem to accept their condition as a fate against which nothing could prevail.

In all this, where do I stand today?

For a while I thought that my conflicts were resolved *in* my writings, *by* my writings. I remember having written somewhere that my books (of poetry and prose) were, are, the houses that I inhabit. It's true. And it looks simple. And it is not. Even here the harbor is not safe from trouble.

Expatriate or exiled writers find in their condition a perspective on their original countries and on themselves which they may have not found had they stayed "home." The examples in contemporary literature alone are numerous, and telling: Rilke, Hemingway, Gertrude Stein . . . to name a few, or Joyce (or, in painting, Picasso). Writing (or art) seem to be the only meaningful activity when one is uprooted: it gives form and substance to what otherwise would be a devouring chaos.

But while the expatriate can still, and *does* function within the literary tradition and historical continuity of his or her own country, the exiled writer usually adopts the language of the country of adoption, and its whole context. In my own case, I have to say that I write in two languages, English and French, neither of them being what should have been my original language, Arabic. Then the crucial question would follow: what do I write and for whom? These are painful problems that writers in exile have to face. There aren't many ways out of marginality. I am an American writer who is also an Arab. I am also an Arab writer who is American. I am home in California. I feel close to some of the American poets I know or whose works I read. I belong to their world too. Some of them (Lyn Hejinian, Barbara Guest . . .) enchant my mind the way the poets (so different from them) I read when I was 18 or 19 (Baudelaire, Rimbaud . . .), while I was in Beirut, and so impatient to read them that I was often sitting on the edge of a sidewalk with their book in my hand. But in me, and in writers who like me function in societies they were not born in, there always is an undercurrent of uncertainty, again a certain distance: for whom are we writing? I always thought and still believe that poetry is essentially tribal, it relates to archetypes, collective memory, communal language and interests. Even the most formal of French poets, the one with greatest influence nowadays on Western poetics, wrote a famous verse (speaking of the function of poetry): *donner un sens plus pur aux mots de la tribu* (to give a purer meaning to the tribe's words). So, for my American readers my references come too often from Arab culture and history, and for my Arab readers the environment of my poetry is the American experience and the American landscape: Who would then follow me through my work?

One thing is certain: I cannot go back "home," the initial home. In other times emigrants couldn't go back because travels were not common and were costly. Today this is not the problem. But Beirut represents a unique case: it does not exist anymore and will not exist, I mean the Beirut I knew. It has been destroyed and will not be rebuilt according to its old patterns. So when I go there I have to look for the street I was born on, the places I used to go to . . . knowing too well that I will never find them again. It is as if when I am there I am not there, and some people could lose their mind for less.

What am I to say? That our illusions concerning the Arab world have been destroyed? Yes. We dreamed of Arab unity while today we have a hard time imagining that any one of those countries will hold together. We believed, against all evidence, that America somehow would become a positive factor, would help the world out of its degradation, but its policies have been rather a recipe for more chaos and devastation.

I came to think—which is no consolation—that our predicament is not only our own. Amidst ecological disaster, economic predatory tactics and political bankruptcy, a human being, wherever, appears to be a fallen angel, an angel exiled from the old Paradise as well as from the future. Exile is not the sad privilege of only a few individuals: it has become synonymous with the human condition, but with (slight) difference that some of us are eaten by this illness in ways evident and definitive while all the others are not yet conscious of what they already are suffering from. We are, as contemporaries of this day and age, all, very, very close to each other, but very few are those who share with us that knowledge.

NOTE ON THIS EDITION

The three essays collected here were written by Etel Adnan in English in the 1980s and '90s and have until now only appeared in journals and anthologies. Patrice Cotensin, editor and publisher of Éditions L'Échoppe, has done a great service in translating these essays into French, along with several other short works by Adnan, and publishing them in separate volumes in an elegant series. I was introduced to these editions while in Paris to work with Simone Fattal shortly after Adnan's death in 2021. Fattal and I then began discussing the need for the texts to appear anew in English. Fattal immediately identified three essays—*Écrire dans une langue étrangère*, *Grandir et devenir poète au Liban*, and *Voyage, guerre, exil*—as texts that should appear in one volume in their original English. The selection of original drawings by Simone Fattal in this new English edition were created for Cotensin's edition of *Grandir et devenir poète au Liban*.

The process of republishing these essays in English has involved some reverse editing, since Adnan made edits to the French text of *Grandir et devenir poète au Liban* (including the title) before publication. Without a record of these edits, I engaged Jérémy Robert for a reading and comparison between the original English essay and the more recent French version. Simone Fattal indicated that we should use the original English title here, and so it appears as "Growing Up to Be a Woman Writer in Lebanon." I have edited these essays with a very light hand retaining, for example, Adnan's use of British spellings while adapting punctuation to the American style. This collection presents meditations on a remarkable biography, recounted kaleidoscopically in Adnan's insightful and poetic prose. What emerges is a testament to a life lived in motion—intellectual, geographic, linguistic and artistic *perpetual* motion—as well as a model for reckoning with and surviving our times of war and exile.

E. Tracy Grinnell
Brooklyn, New York
October 2024

ACKNOWLEDGMENTS

ORIGINAL ENGLISH PUBLICATIONS

"To Write in a Foreign Language." In *Unheard Words: Women and Literature in Africa, the Arab World, Asia, the Carribean, and Latin America*, edited by Mineke Schipper, 247-257. London: Allison & Busby, 1984.

"Growing Up to Be a Woman Writer in Lebanon." *Opening the Gates: A Century of Arab Feminist Writing*, edited by Margot Badran and Myriam Cooke, 5-20. Bloomington: Indiana University Press, 1990.

"Voyage, War, and Exile." *Al-'Arabiyya* 28 (1995): 5-16.

IN TRANSLATION (FRENCH)

Écrire dans une langue étrangère (2015)
Grandir et devenir poète au Liban (2019)
Voyage, guerre, exil (2020)

Translated by Patrice Cotensin
Éditions L'Échoppe

ORIGINAL ARTWORK

Cover art and drawings by Simone Fattal, created for the French publication *Grandir et devenir poète au Liban* (Éditions L'Échoppe, 2019).

Cover image: "Untitled," 2019. Ink on watercolor paper. 25.5 x 15.5cm.

Endpages image: "Forest," 2019. Ink on paper. 44 x 55 cm.

Interior image 1 (page 9): "Untitled," 2019. Ink on watercolor paper. 31.5 x 24 cm.

Interior image 2 (page 33): "Untitled," 2019. Ink on watercolor paper. 45 x 30 cm.

Interior image 3 (page 67): "Untitled," 2019. Ink on watercolor paper. 31 x 24 cm.

ETEL ADNAN (1925-2021) was born in Beirut, Lebanon. She is a celebrated writer, essayist, poet, and playwright, and is the author of more than twenty books in all these disciplines. Her work as a whole is a faithful record of the times and places she has lived in Beirut, Paris, and in the San Francisco Bay Area. At least eighteen works by Adnan have been published in English. They include *Sitt Marie Rose* (Post-Apollo Press, 1982); *The Arab Apocalypse* (Post-Apollo Press, 1989); *Sea and Fog* (Nightboat Books, 2012), winner of the Lambda Literary Award for Lesbian Poetry and the California Book Award for Poetry; *Premonition* (Kelsey Street Press, 2014); *Surge* (Nightboat Books, 2018); *Time* (Nightboat Books, 2019), winner of the Griffin Poetry Prize and the Best Translated Book Award; *Shifting the Silence* (Nightboat Books, 2020); and most recently, a second edition of *Journey to Mount Tamalpais* (Litmus Press, 2021), which includes nine new ink drawings by Adnan and an afterword by Omar Berrada. Her paintings, described by New York Times art critic Roberta Smith as "stubbornly radiant abstractions," have been widely exhibited. Spanning media and genres, Adnan's writings have led to numerous collaborations with artists and musicians, including the French part of CIVIL warS, a multi-language opera by American stage director Robert Wilson, performed in Lyon and Bobigny in 1985.

In 2014 she was named Chevalier des Arts et des Lettres, France's highest cultural honor, by the French Government.

Born in Damascus, Syria, artist and writer SIMONE FATTAL grew up in Lebanon and studied philosophy at Beirut's École des lettres and Paris' Sorbonne. Returning to Beirut in 1969, she began creating paintings and sculptures in a small live-in studio. In 1980, Fattal relocated to Sausalito, California with Etel Adnan. There, she founded The Post-Apollo Press, a publisher devoted to innovative and experimental literary work. In 1988, she returned to artistic practice by doing ceramic sculptures after enrolling at the Art Institute of San Francisco. Since 2006, she has produced works in Hans Spinner's prestigious workshop in Grasse, France. In 2013, she released a movie, *Autoportrait*, which has been shown worldwide in many film festivals.

Simone Fattal lives and works in Paris. She is the 2024 recipient of the Berlin Grand Art Prize, Julio González International Prize, and the Rosa Schapire Art Prize.

Forest
nov 2019 / attaf.